Gulls off Schoodic Point

Overleaf (2-3): Mount Desert Island *Overleaf (4-5):* Seawall Beach, Phippsburg

Photographing Coastal Maine

My first plane ride was in a tri-motored Ford when I was five years old. Folks would call the aircraft an antique nowadays — the year, 1936. Suddenly I saw the world from a whole new perspective and my eyes were popping as I looked down on toy towns, tiny railroads and miniature farm lands. I've never forgotten the thrill of that first flight and considering how few people actually got aloft in those days, mine was a special privilege indeed. So, when I was asked to photograph *Coastal Maine* I found myself guided by nostalgia from those impressions that molded my youth. I concluded, the best way to portray Maine's intricate slivers of land, hidden coves and myriad of islands, was by air.

As with any project like this book there is a story behind every photograph — each a mini-adventure where old friends and new ones are encountered along the way. Some moments are particularly strong but those incomparable mornings when I was in a plane at dawn skimming over harbor towns with church steeples and ships masts poking up through veils of fog . . . or tops of bright colored Autumn trees seemingly bubbling from the mist like balloons, is pure magic.

If you were to stretch Maine's entire coastline out in a straight line it would run several thousand miles. Even from the air its fractured features are enough to make you gasp with astonishment. It is my hope that those aerial views within this book will provide an elucidating glimpse of this remarkable shoreline. I'm indebted to those pilots who cranked up their craft in the blackness of dawn so that I might capture the magic on film. Also, I would like to thank many kind friends who helped with suggestions and accommodations in making this book possible. And to dependable Nikon cameras and lenses along with Kodachrome 64 film from which all the photographs were shot.

But most of all, I am grateful to my publisher for without his continued faith in my work none of this would have been possible. In the final analysis a photographer's efforts are no better than the talents and genius of the editor whose task is to pull the collection of film together in a workable layout flowing from page to page. It has been a privilege for me to share this partnership with my friend and editor, James B. Patrick.

Clyde H. Smith

Credits

Photographs © copyright 1985 Clyde H. Smith.

Copyright © 1985 Foremost Publishers, Inc.

This book, or portions thereof, may not be reproduced in any form without the permission of Foremost Publishers, Inc. Photographs may not be reproduced in any form without the permission of Clyde H. Smith.

Edited by James B. Patrick.

Designed by Donald G. Paulhus.

Printed in Japan

ISBN 0-89909-085-0

Published by Foremost Publishers, Inc.
An affiliate of Yankee Publishing Inc.
Dublin, New Hampshire 03444

Coastal MAINE

Photography by Clyde H. Smith
Introduction by John Gould

Published by Foremost Publishers, Inc.
An Affiliate of Yankee Publishing Inc.

Coastal Maine

There's so much to tell about Coastal Maine! Here, between the Isles of Shoals and Fundy Bay, were the beginnings of everything we think of as America; three thousand miles of history, romance, adventure, intrigue, scenery, and a breed of down-Mainers consistent with the geography they love. That many miles? Yes — you can sooner walk from New York to San Francisco than you can perambulate (Perambulate! that's a good Maine word for stepping right along) the shoreline of Maine. Should you walk the Maine coast, you'd still have hundreds of islands left over. Maine's tidal edge runs to more distance than all the rest of our Atlantic coast from Pull-and-be-damned Point to Key West. And it was landfall for America at least four hundred years before Columbus was born (probably in Genoa).

The history books like to teach us that piety, probity, and a big yen for freedom prompted the praying Pilgrims to move in and give us a sturdy legacy of upright conduct and proper philosophies. But when those Pilgrims decided to come to America, they asked the proprietors of Maine, already in business, for permission to settle there. These gentlemen, hardnosed investors, thought about that and concluded the intrusion of free-thinkers into their workaday fish business might prove a disturbing influence, so they said no. They suggested the Pilgrims take their piety more to the south — Massachusetts perhaps. But on their way by, when they finally came, the Pilgrims paused at Monhegan Island to "take some coddes," and in after years when they were hungry they remembered that and came back to Maine for more fish. Later still, when the Pilgrims tried to establish trading stations along our Kennebec River, they showed poor business aptitude and the venture failed.

But just about everybody else who tried to exploit Coastal Maine made out dandy. For a great many years Europeans had been fishing "The Bank" without paying too much attention to the mainland (the maine) which they could see from their decks. The fish they caught were cured in brine aboard ship and taken home for sale when the hold was full. Somewhere around the time Columbus told Isabella the world was round, one of these fishermen had a bright idea. Why not take these fish ashore while still fresh, cut and cure them, and send them to Europe in dry salt? Much easier to handle and a neater cargo. In a few years fisheries stations ashore (mostly on islands) were active, and there developed a keen competition which (as far as this story matters) settled into a French-English economic hassle. England was still bringing back the "soft cure" of fish in brine, and France was offering a salt-slacked dry codfish which was superior. When the English finally woke up, the scattered fisheries of France were centered at Ste. Croix and St. Saviour, and France claimed Maine.

One of the first good descriptions of Maine came in 1553 when a French writer named Thêvet came over to give a look. His book is extant. At one place he tells about sailing into our Penobscot Bay and coming to a place "where the French formerly had a fort." Interesting wording. Forts are meant to protect people and investments, and in 1553 here was a fort so old that Thêvet used the word *autrefois*. The logs had rotted away and trees had grown over the spot. How long since the fort was built? We can well wish that Thêvet had told us more about early French activities on Penobscot Bay, but we can be glad he did give us good descriptions of Coastal Maine. It would be a full half century later that an English writer did the same.

When the English did wake up, King James made a grant, and in 1605 the gentlemen incorporators of his trading company sent Captain George Waymouth in his ship *Archangel* to find suitable locations for English settlements. With Waymouth was James Rosier, scribe of the expedition. Rosier's job was to describe Maine so volunteers back home would be enticed to sign up and move to Maine to handle fish. Until that time, Posier had been a second-rate hack and his prose had shown little talent. But suddenly, with one look at the "land of the pointed firs" and one whiff of clean Maine air, he blossomed. Maine, he wrote, was so beautiful he couldn't begin to tell . . . Each scene he described was amazingly improved by the next. Proof of his success was immediate recruitment of some hundred and fifty eager colonists. Men were carried away by the charming rhetoric of Maine's first tub-thumper; glad to be off to Rosier's Paradise.

The coast of Maine does have an effect on writers. Thêvet and Rosier proliferated into scores of authors and poets to continue their work. Kenneth Roberts, one of the authors, marveled that so many wing-ed words could be inspired thus. He listed Maine writers (*Trending into Maine*, 1938) and suggested students of American literature give heed. Sarah Orne Jewett, Edwin Arlington Robinson, Harriet Beecher Stowe, Robert Peter Tristram Coffin, Edna St. Vincent Millay, Harold T. Pulsifer, Mary Ellen Chase, Lincoln Colcord, Booth Tarkington, Henry Wadsworth Longfellow . . . his list filled better than a page of his book and he missed many. Well, add Ruth Moore and Elisabeth Ogilvie, for two, and Ken Roberts was too early to know about Stephen King. Too bad; wouldn't it be good to have an opinion about Steve King from Ken Roberts?

The literary accumulation of down-Maine writers has had ample pictorial support from artists. Comes to mind, first, Charles Woodbury at Ogunquit, who is still quoted for his admonition to his students that "rocks shouldn't float." He taught many young artists well, and nobody ever counted the canvases they did of Ogunquit's surf and sea. Interestingly, his son David didn't take to art, but became a Maine writer that Kenneth Roberts missed. Then there was Winslow Homer at Prouts Neck; there was N. C. Wyeth, son and grandson. But any attempt to list Maine artists will bring to mind the start of the Boston Marathon; they came and they still come and there are more. On Monhegan Island, artists work in shifts, for want of room to stand hip by hip and see the scenery. Alta Ashley, today's Monhegan Island scribe, tallies arriving artists by counting easels on the deck of the boat "from the main" when it arrives.

But nobody counts cameras. The incomparable Chansonetta Stanley Emmons was offering views of Coastal Maine early in this century — using dry plates invented by her brothers (they also invented the Stanley Steamer). Chansonetta (tch! tch!) even made some seaside female nudes! In 1959 *Maine Coastal Portrait* appeared, with black and white pictures made by Jim Moore, Kosti Ruohomaa, and Carroll Thayer Berry. Very nice. But in 1980, when Arthur Griffin, "New England's Photographer Laureate," produced his color-picture book, *Four Seasons*, he felt Coastal Maine had been photographed at the expense of inland Maine, and he pretty much opted instead for "highlander" views — lakes and mountains and farmland. But Coastal Maine is nevertheless ready, willing, and waiting to be posed again — quiet in summer calm; outraged by winter no'theasters; bright under a high sun or drenched by clinging fog; inviting to vacation picnickers but warily respected by laconic lobster catchers; blue now and grimly gray-green again. The home of a special person — the down-Mainer who never says yes and never says no.

Mainers have a lingo. It derives from their Scot-Irish-English origins, with transfusions by times, their experiences through the years, and the nature of Coastal Maine. Some years ago the bureaucrats in Washington decided the Maine lobster fishermen had been frugal in their tax payments. There was a big investigation, during which the fiscal customs of Coastal Maine were deplored by government experts, and as a consequence a number of honest, upright, and "aggervated" Mainers were indicted for crimes and misdemeanors. There were no crimes and misdemeanors; only a failure on the part of Washington to understand Coastal Maine. The battery of smart young lawyers sent up here to teach our boys a lesson made a formidable array before the presiding justice, who was a native of Maine, and after some opening statements witnesses were called. To a question, one of the lobstermen responded, "Eyah, you might say so." The attorney parried for a better answer, but as he badgered the witness the judge interrupted with, "That's enough — the question has been answered."

Later, to another question, another lobsterman replied, "Daow!" Daow is a down-Maine coastal emphatic which means no only moreso. It will certainly be used if in any way a question can be construed as absurd. When the word came out, the judge looked at the government lawyers with a big smile, and before one of them spoke he said, "The question has been answered."

There have been intrusions into Maine speech by the generalizing of an "American" language by movies, radio, and television, and there have been influences from summer people (summercaters who retire to Maine are winterizers). But the true strain survives, and must be heard in its native lair. The words can be spelled and the expressions put in books, but such efforts are glass flowers that have no smell. The imagery and the poetry require a voice. Did you ever try to carry water in a basket? That's why we call a gossiping old woman a basket. "Her? That one — she's a reg'lar old barskit; can't keep a secret ten minutes." Eyah. There is something magnificently wonderful about a battery of smart young Washington lawyers crowding into chambers to have the judge explain what "Daow!" means.

Maine coastal people, like the button on the backhouse door, have been around. Coming by sea to live by the sea, they stayed with the sea through the great days of down-east seafaring, until steam licked the sail. Whole towns went to sea. Every dooryard built ships. Neighbors from home "gammed" in the ports of Marseilles, Calcutta, Liverpool, Rio. A captain who carried his family kept a "hen frigate," and many a Maine child was named for his birthplace — Andaman Islands Scholfield, Montevideo Gott, Marseilles Bibber, Leeward Toothaker. Toothaker was called "Loo," because Mainers say looward for leeward — The Loo'ard Islands. And after the Civil War, to which Maine sent a greater proportion of its population than any other northern state, many of our soldiers moved west and took up homesteads. When Hollywood pictures a Montana cowpoke of the late 1800s speaking with a Montana drawl, the humor is there — the Montana cowpoke of the late 1800s was probably from Rockland, Maine, used eyah and daow, and probably was hungry for a good feed of codfish balls. Anyway, Mainers were never strangers to the great wide world, and have retained their personalities and their speech as quaint and curious localisms. Everybody else is from away.

Enjoy! Coastal Maine has been pleasing people for a long, long time.

John Gould

Pemaquid Point Light, erected 1827

13   Janquish and Bailey Islands

Firehouse turned giftshop in Damariscotta

Sunset, South Harpswell

Net – mending at West Point Harbor

Overleaf: East Boothbay

Mildly concerned harbor seals

The "Heritage", at foggy Fox Island Thorofare

Patriotism on Great Gott Island

Overleaf: Camden and harbor

28   Eagle Lake, Mount Desert Island

29   Apple orchard visitor, Swans Island

31   Hockamock Head Light, Swans Island

A fresh effort on Swans Island

Overleaf: Portland Head Light and Ram Island Ledge Light at dawn

Securing day's end, South Bristol

38   Great Pond, Mount Desert Island

Busy day at Sand Beach, Acadia National Park

Kennebec River drawbridge, Bath

41   "Bluenose" at landing in Frenchman Bay, Bar Harbor

Overleaf: "Angelique" in Fox Island Thorofare, North Haven Island

Neighbors, Vinalhaven Island

Topsham sugarmaple

Congregational Church, North Edgecomb

Overleaf: Boothbay Harbor

Stonington Harbor, Deer Isle

Beginning the work day at Burntcoat Harbor

Christmas Cove toward "Thread of Life Ledges"

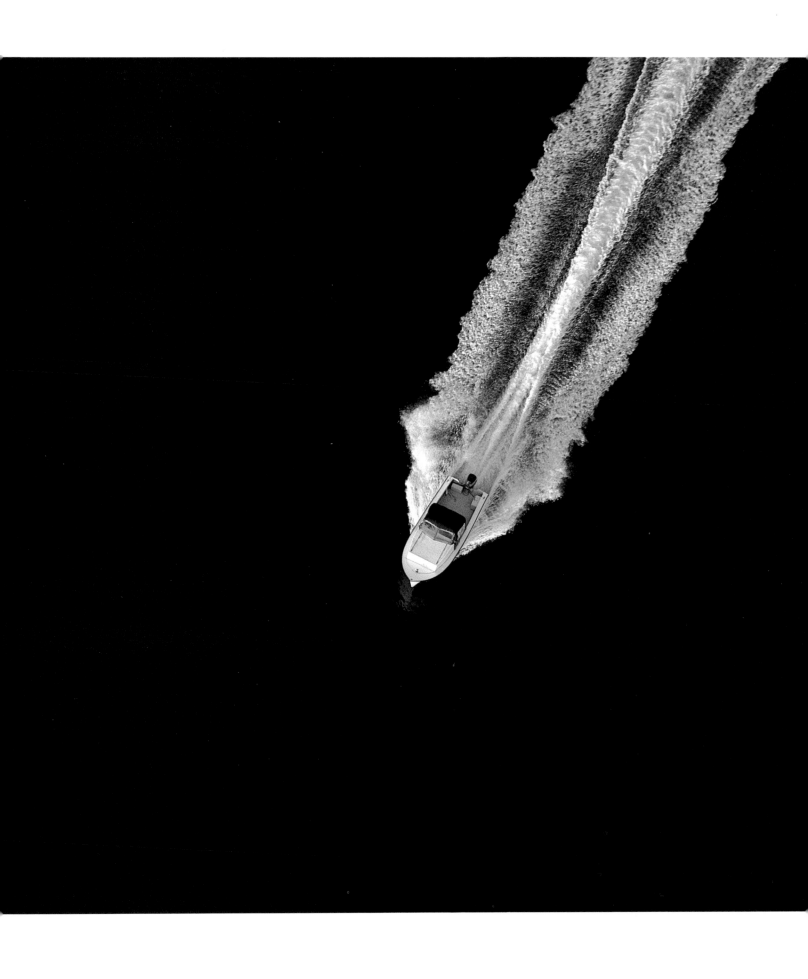

Welder at Goudy & Stevens boat yard, East Boothbay

Goudy & Stevens shipbuilders, with near-complete "Long Liner" in background

Overleaf: Androscoggin River in spring flood, Topsham

Halfway Rock Light, in Casco Bay

"Victory Chimes", largest American passenger-sailing vessel. Built in 1900

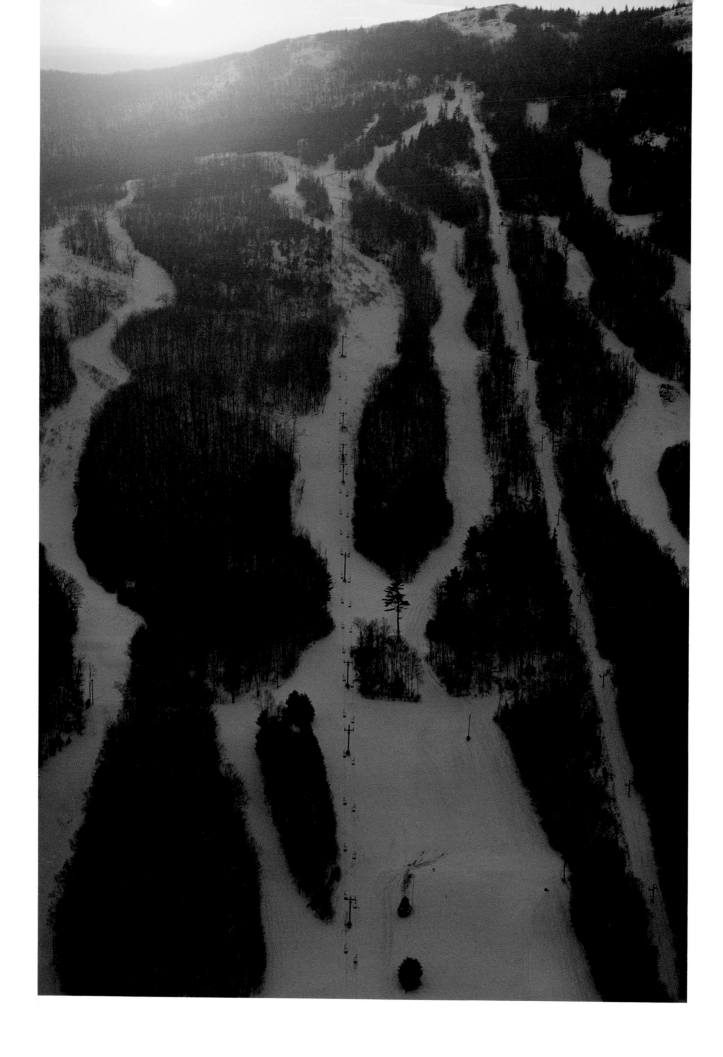

Camden Hills ski area

Swans Island – Hockamock Head Light

Overleaf: Bar Harbor, through morning fog

Wiscasset village on the Sheepscot River

Wiscasset

Bicyclists hitching a ride at North Haven Island

Others prepare to board

Overleaf: Shorebirds feeding at low tide

Lightning strikes beyond Cape Neddick Nubble Light, York

73 Coastal schooner anchors at Owls Head Harbor

Tenants Harbor

Heavy surf at Cape Neddick

Overleaf: Autumn carpet surrounds deserted farmhouse on Deer Isle

Navy ship at Bath Iron Works on the Kennebec

"Piper" in Vinalhaven

Overleaf: Foggy morning near Damariscotta countryside

Low tide on North Haven Island

Anticipation and curiosity in Port Clyde

Marshall Point Light at Port Clyde

Monhegan Island cliffs, White Head looking toward Black Head

View of eastern promenade – Portland

The Narrows: Kennebec River at outlet of Merrymeeting Bay

Overleaf: Blue Hill Bay

Rockland ferry and North Haven Island yacht club

Old schoolhouse in Castine, now housing private apartments

Owls Head Light, near Rockland

Bald Porcupine Island, Frenchman Bay

Wicker and wood along US Route 1

Overleaf: Muscongus Bay

Southwest Harbor, Mount Desert Island

Vehicles of expression on North Haven Island

Shipshape at Fox Island Thorofare, North Haven Island

Overleaf: Frenchman Bay and Porcupine Islands from Mount Desert Island

Passamaquoddy Bay – Lubec, Maine (left) and Campobello Island, Canada (right)

Lone gull soars off Monhegan Island cliffs

"Bluenose" at landing in Bar Harbor

Mount Desert Narrows at East Lamoine

Days Ferry village on the Kennebec River

Overleaf: Dawn, Boothbay Harbor

Landing at Monhegan Island

Mackerel Cove, Bailey Island

Frosted patches in Merrymeeting Bay

Bowdoinham

Industrious recreation on York Beach

Plimoth Plantation's "Mayflower II" at drydock in Boothbay

Fishing off Schoodic Point, Acadia National Park

Skeletal remains of coastal schooner, "E. T. Willard – 1895"

Calm activity in Eastport Harbor

Portland Head Light